Wrenley's Babies Love The ABC's of CrossFit

*An unofficial parody

Written by Shannon Hunter

Illustrated by Anne Zimanski

For the most supportive and encouraging husband, who is always motivating me to follow my dreams. This book would not be possible without you!

For my boys, not only to be a strong mama, but a fit one too!

A special thank you to my CrossFit Waterside Family and my Coach Cassidy Lance-McWherter!

Copyright © 2021 by Shannon Hunter

All rights reserved. This book or any portion thereof may not be reproduced or used in any manner whatsoever without the express written permission of the publisher except for the use of brief quotations in a book review.

This book is an unofficial parody. CrossFit® is a registered trademark owned by CrossFit, LLC and CrossFit, LLC in no way endorses, sanctions, or supports the contents of the book or any opinions expressed therein.

Printed in the United States of America

First Printing, 2021

ISBN: 978-0-578-90125-1

Aa is for:

Air Squats

Assault Bike

A.M.R.A.P
As Many Rounds
As Possible

Adaptive Athlete

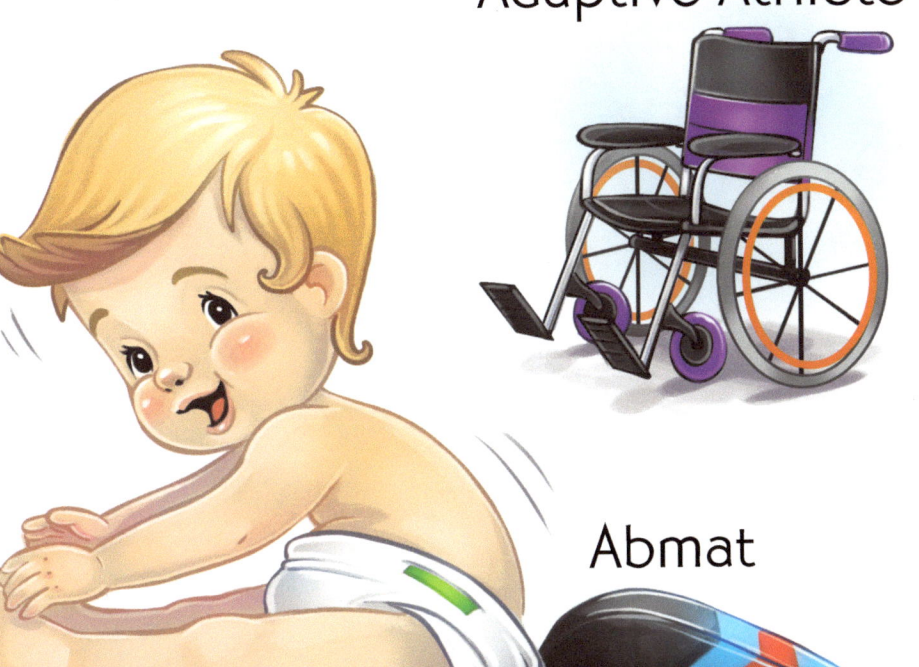

Athlete

Abmat

Cc is for: CrossFit

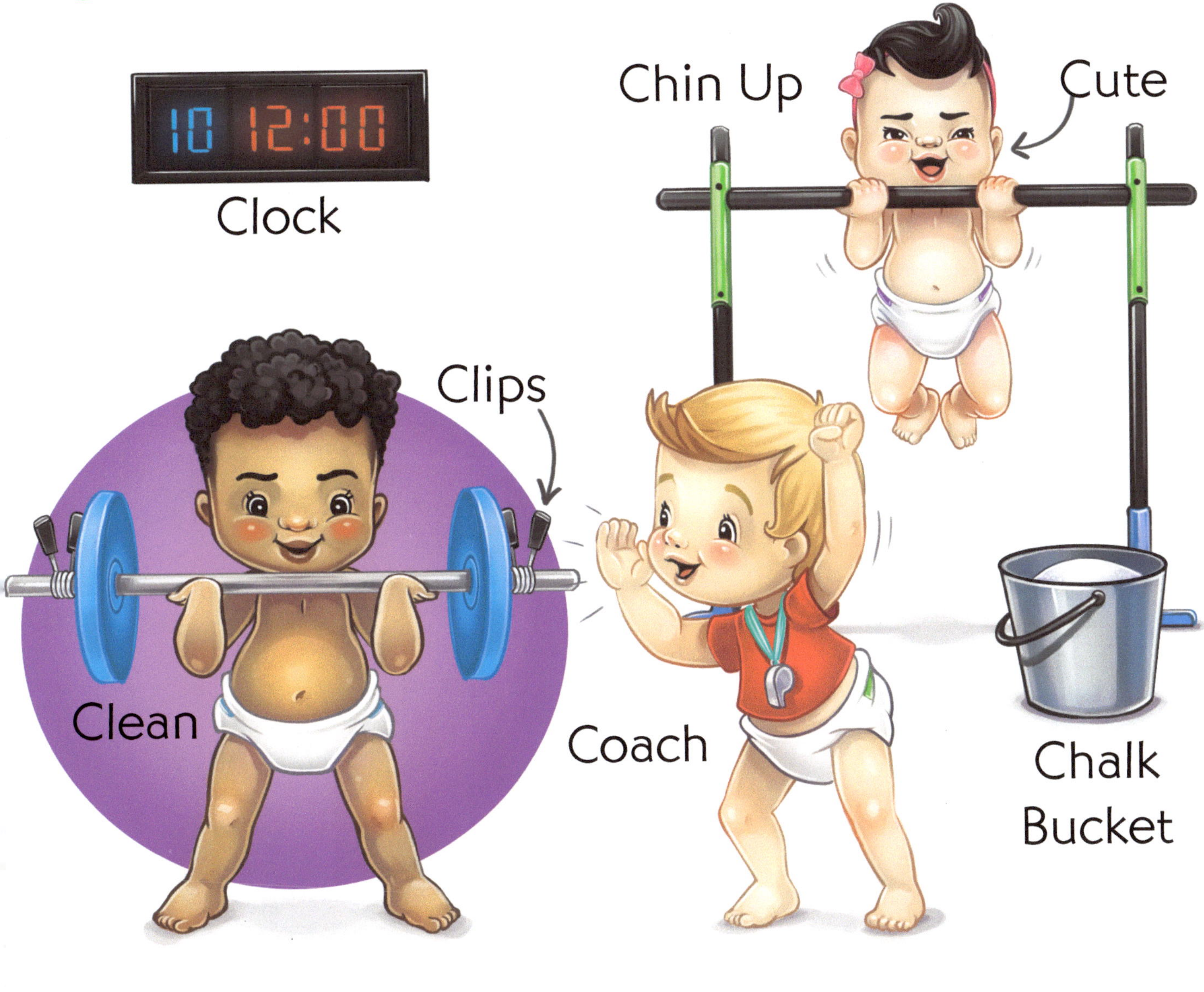

10 12:00
Clock
Chin Up
Cute
Clips
Clean
Coach
Chalk Bucket

Ee is for:

E.M.O.M.
Every Minute On The Minute

Exercise

Energy

Eek!

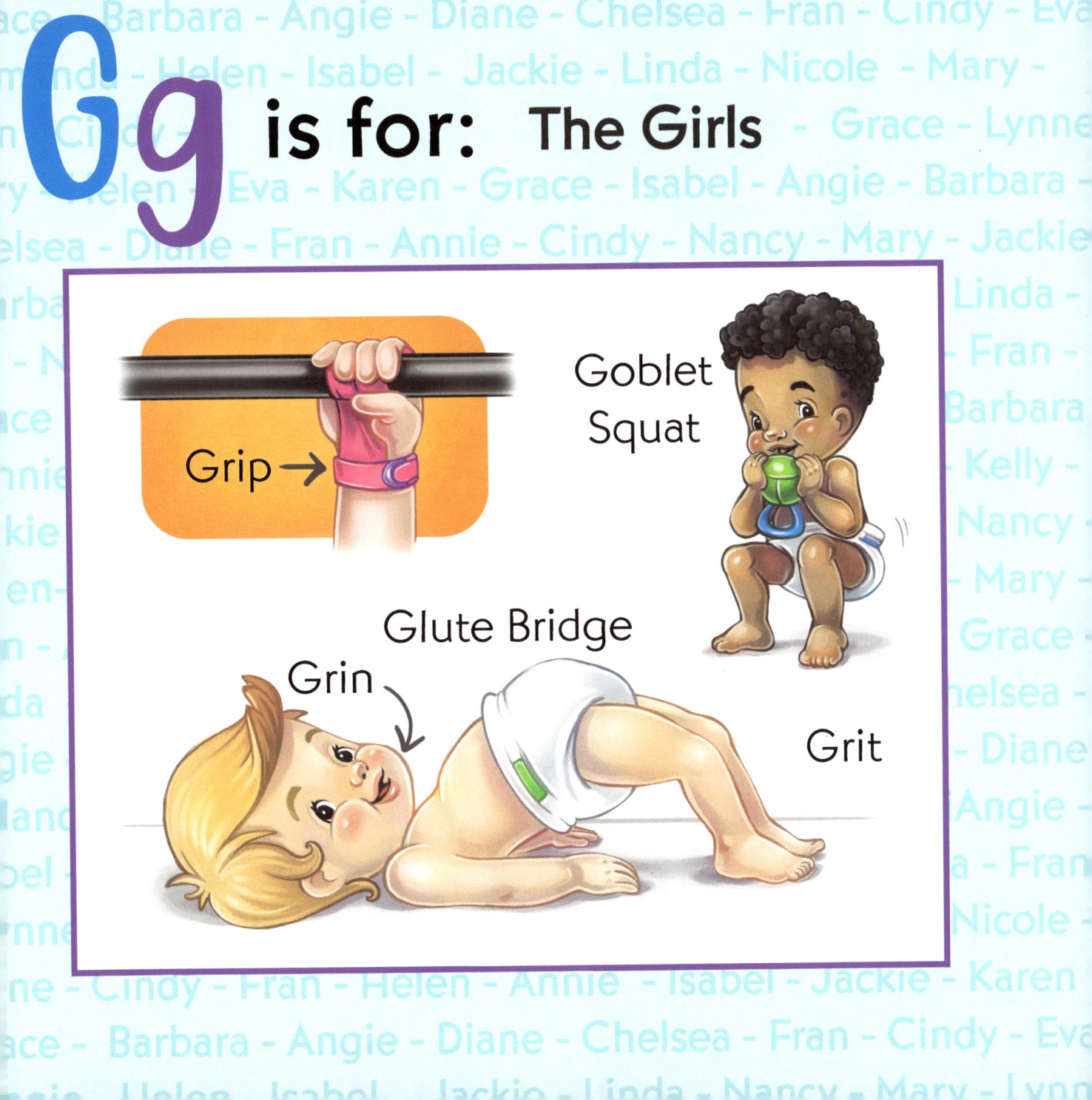

I i is for:

Intervals

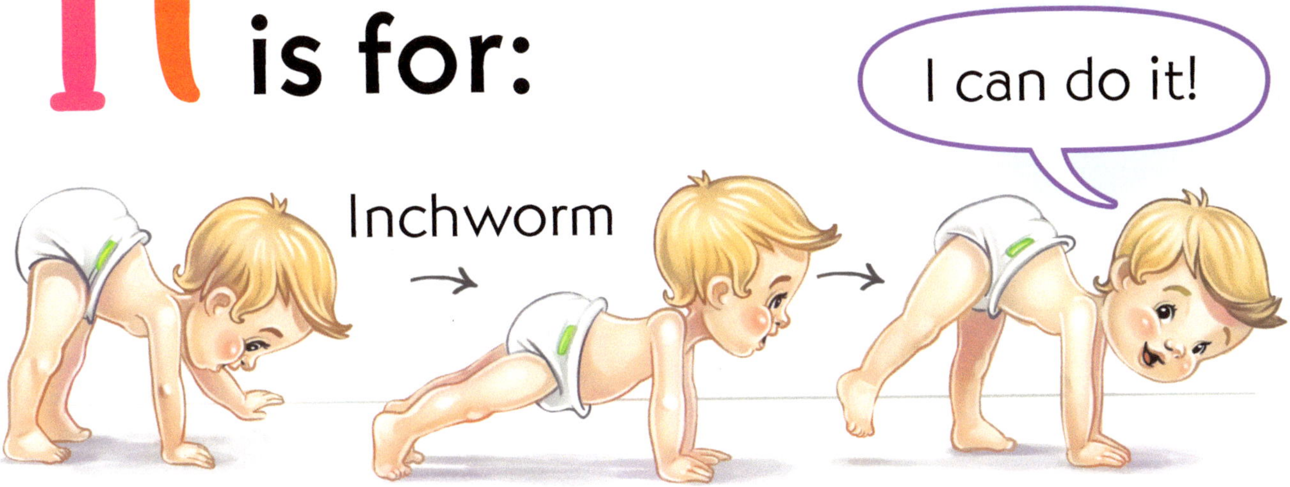

Inchworm

"I can do it!"

J j is for:

Jump Rope

Jumping Lunges

Joy

Judge

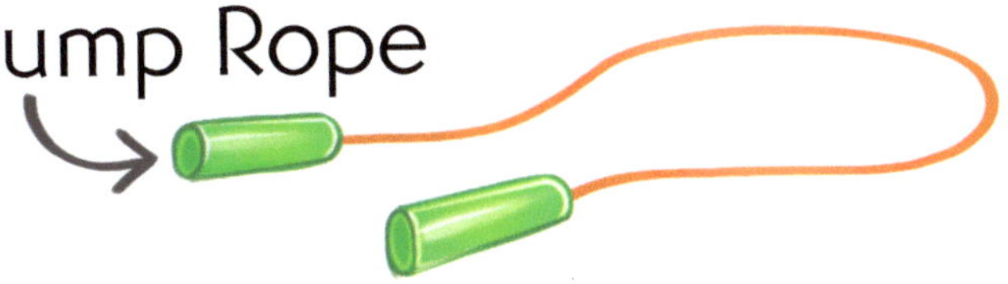

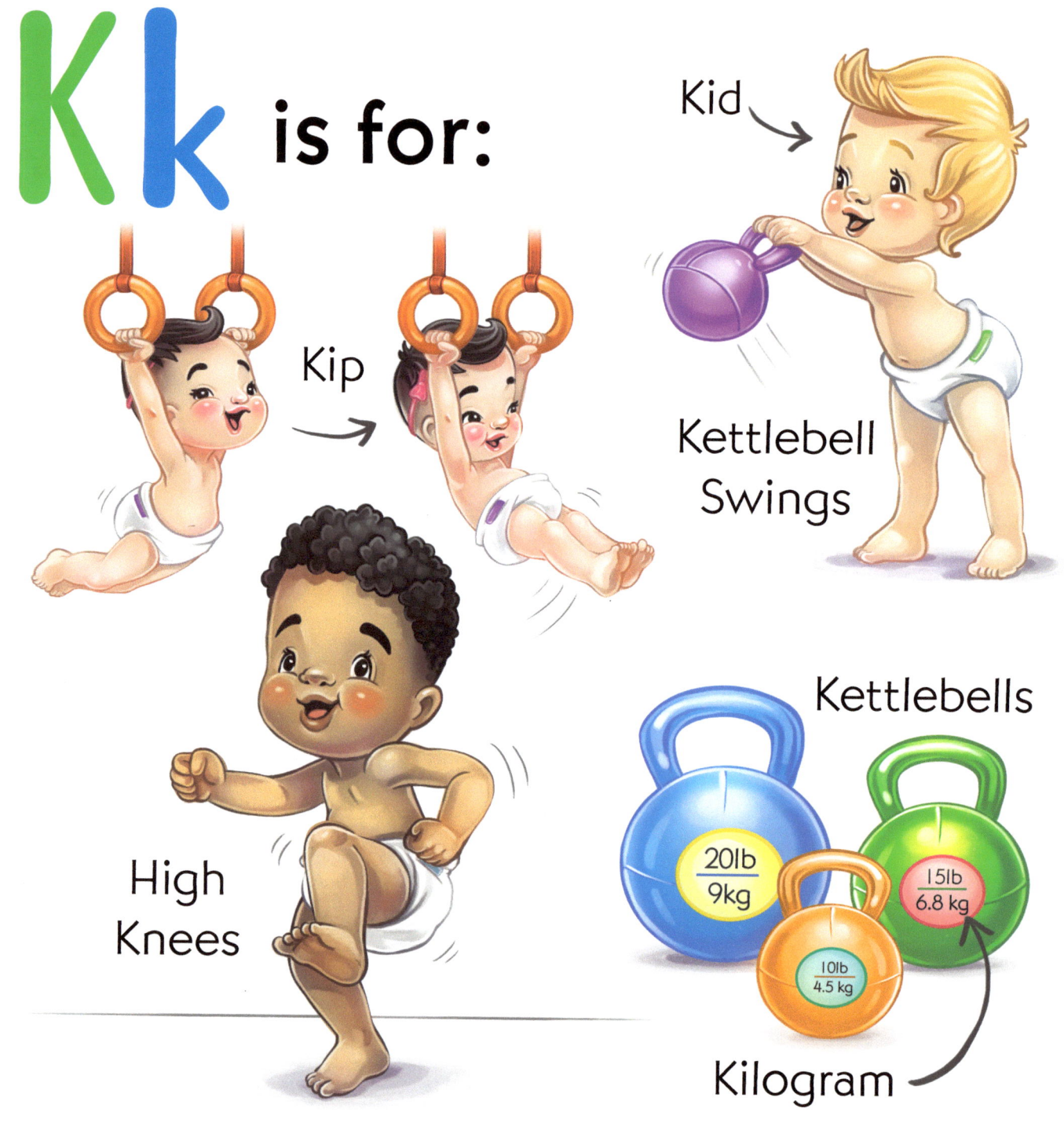

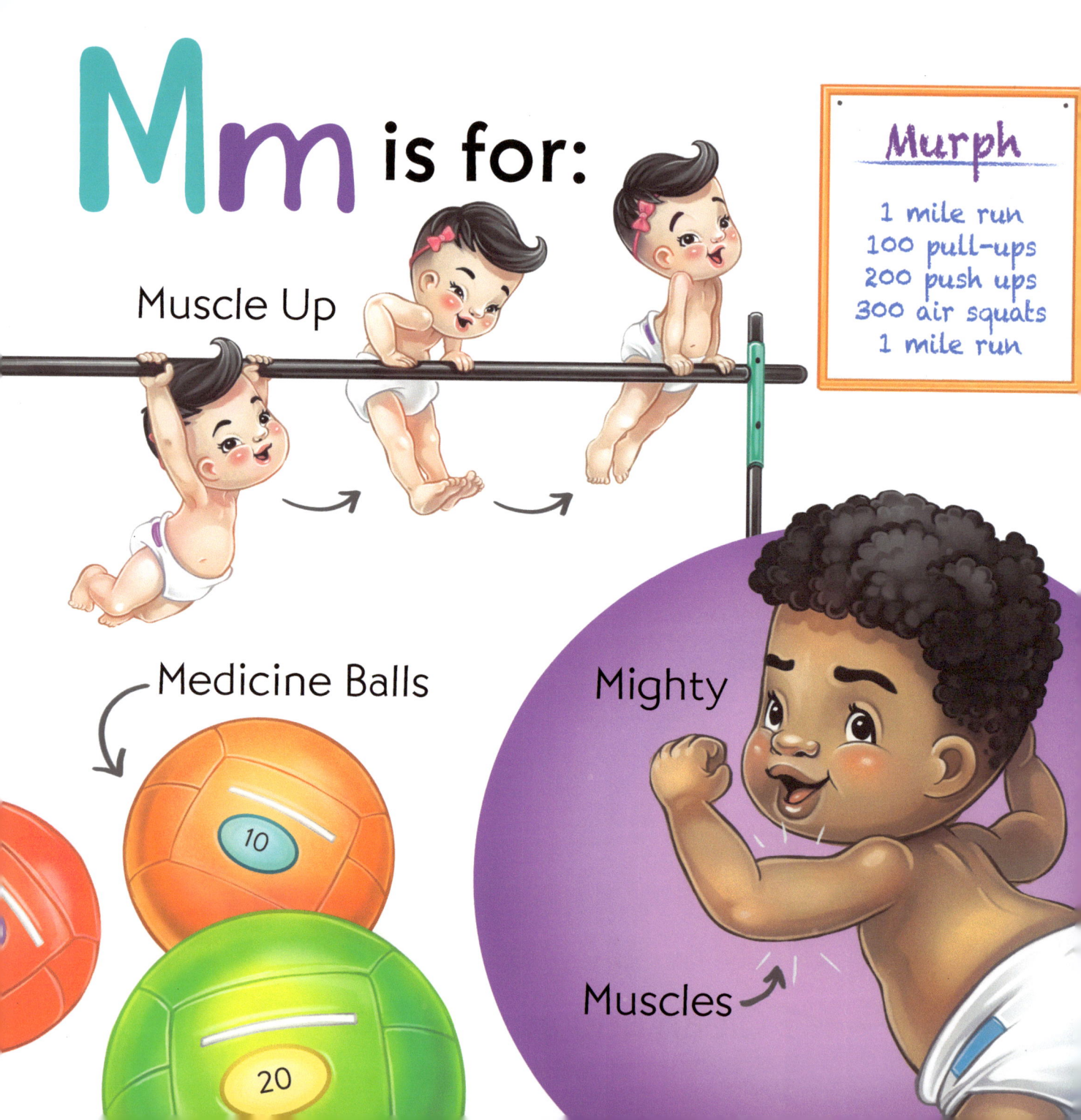

Nn is for:

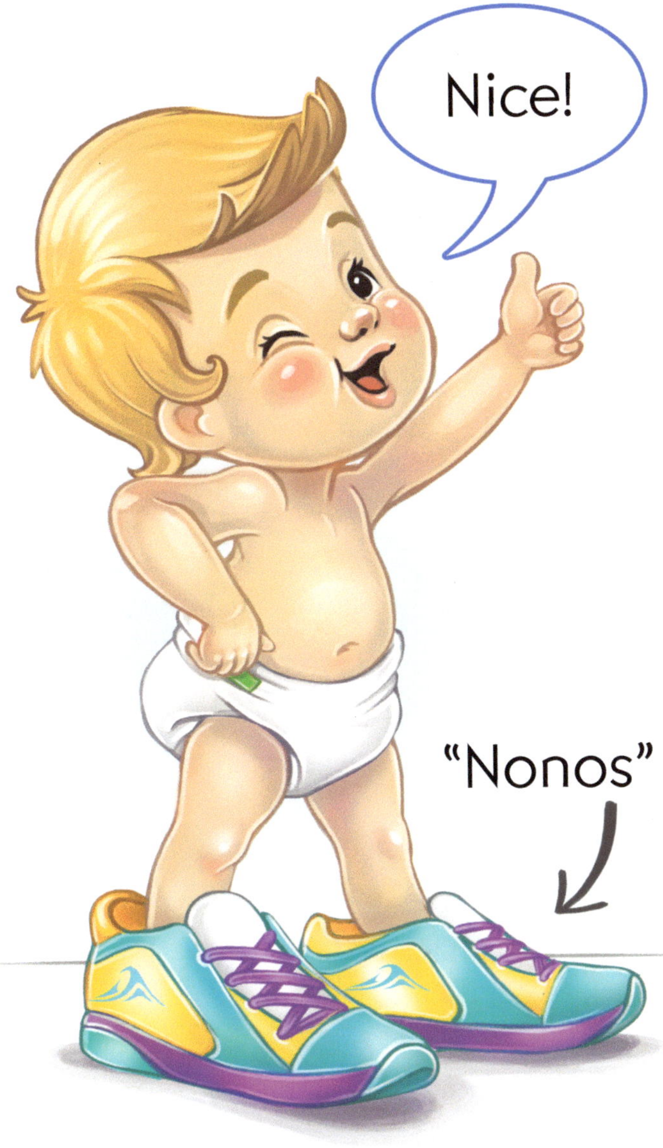
Nice!
"Nonos"

Today's WOD
21
15
Nine

Nutrition
PROTEIN

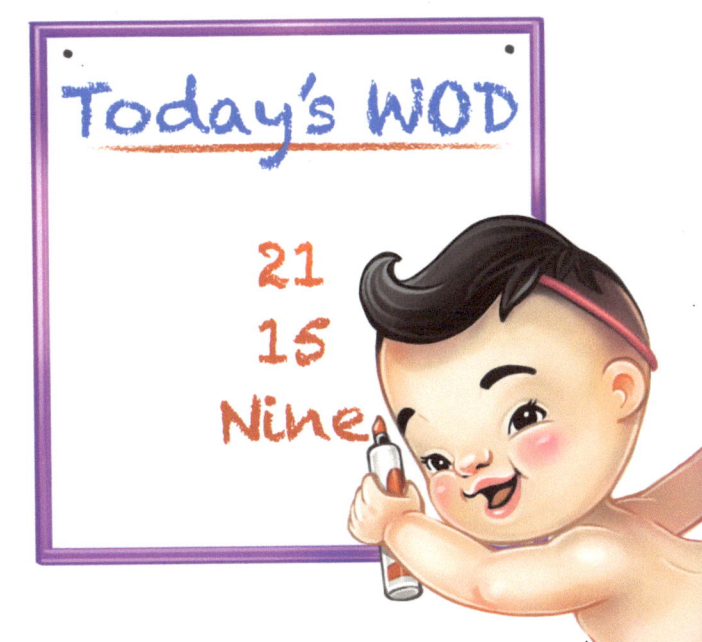

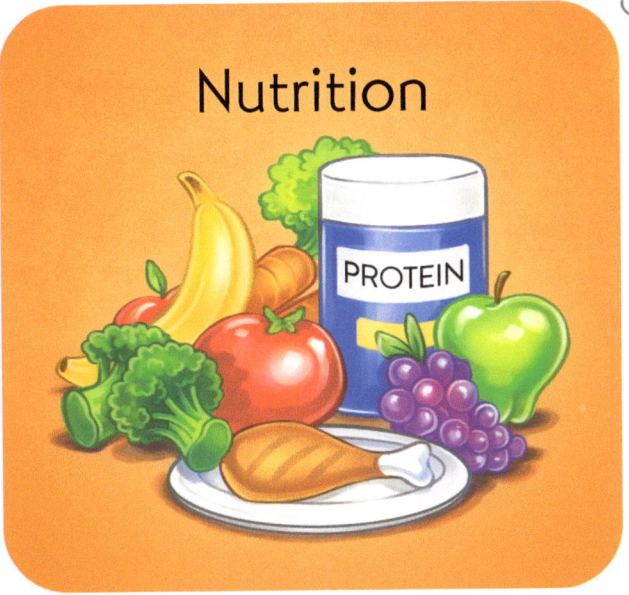

Oo is for:

Olympic Lifting

One Arm Thrusters

Overhead Squat

Oh yeah!

Obliques

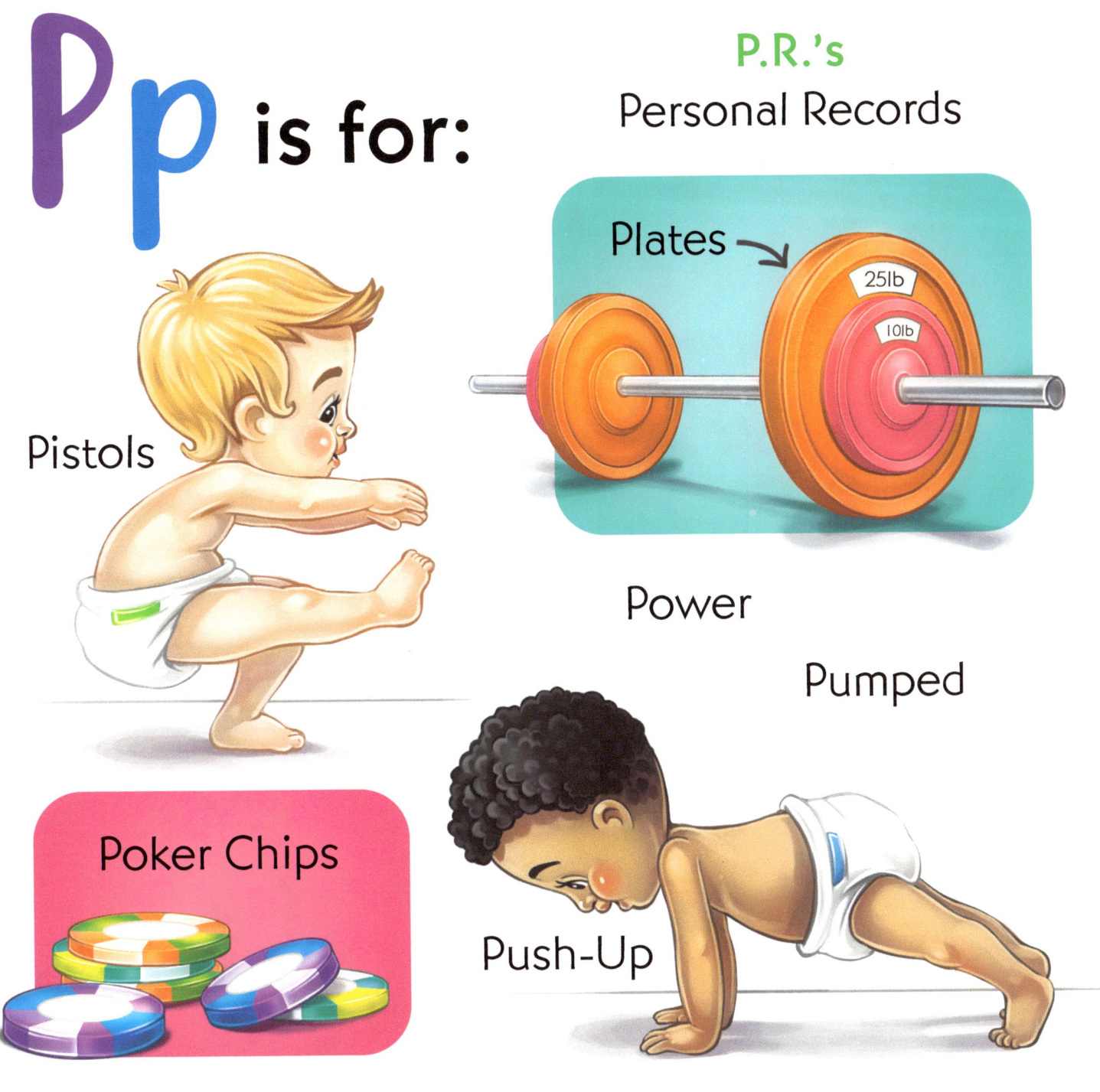

Ss is for:

Sled

Stretch

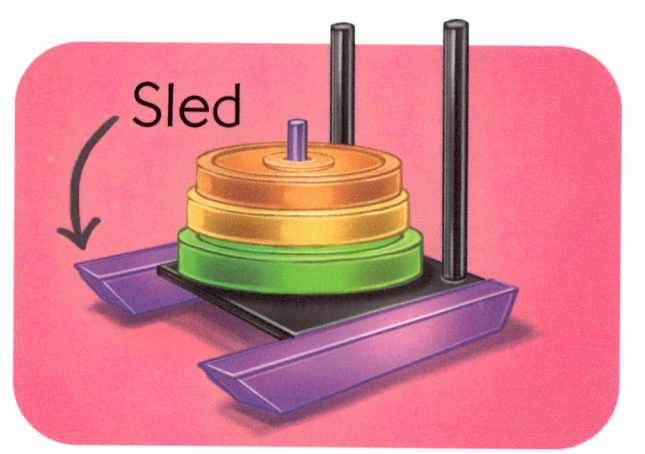

Sets

Sweat

Snatch

Squat

Tt is for:

Toes-to-Bar

Tire

Training

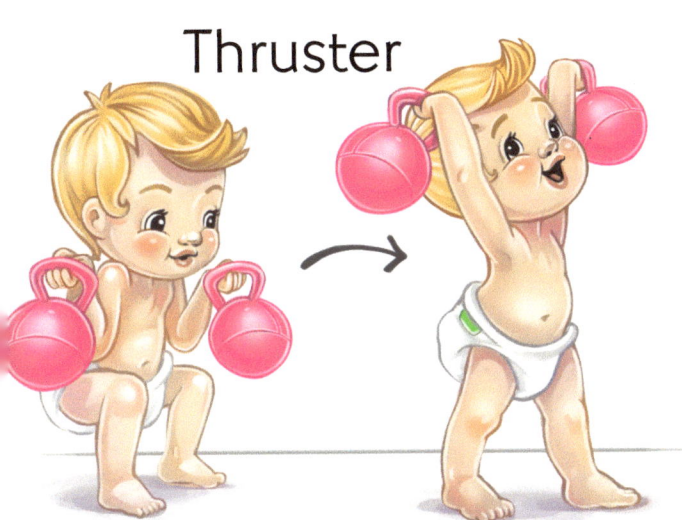
Thruster

Turkish Get-Up

Uu is for:

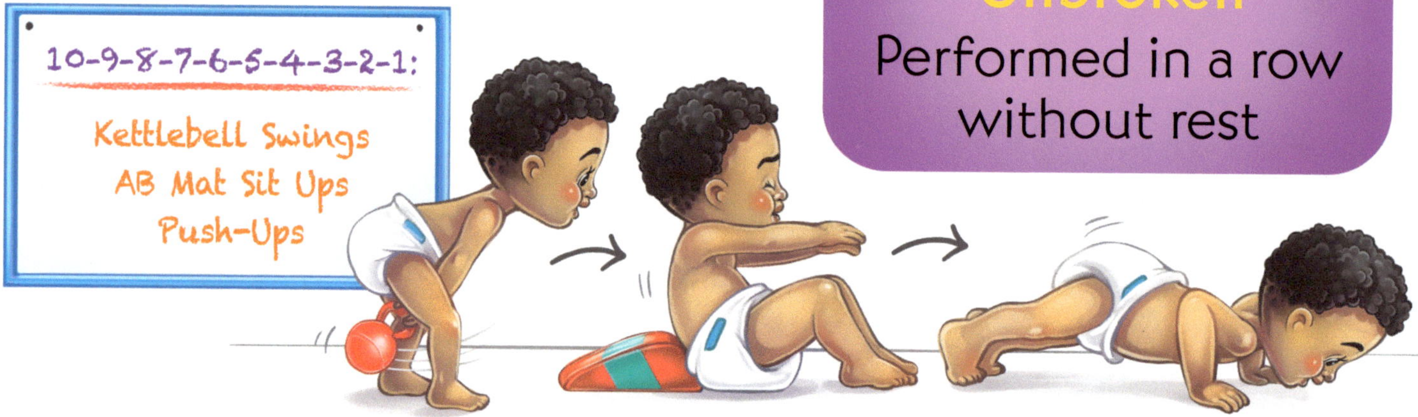

10-9-8-7-6-5-4-3-2-1:
Kettlebell Swings
AB Mat Sit Ups
Push-Ups

Unbroken

Performed in a row without rest

Vv is for:

V-Ups

Fittest
Second
Third

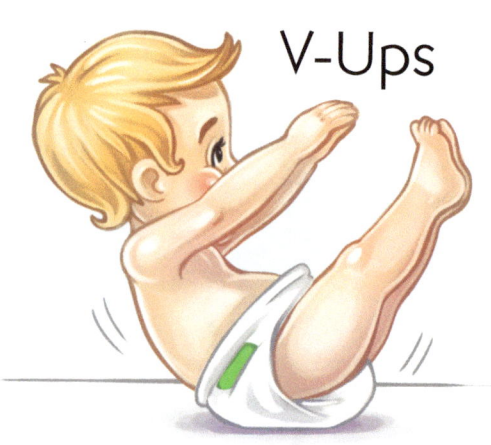

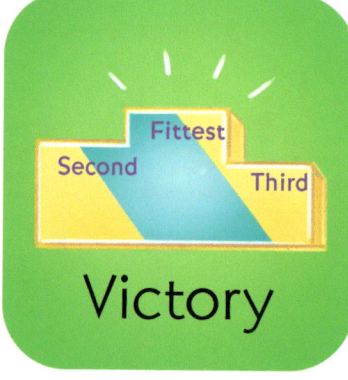

Victory

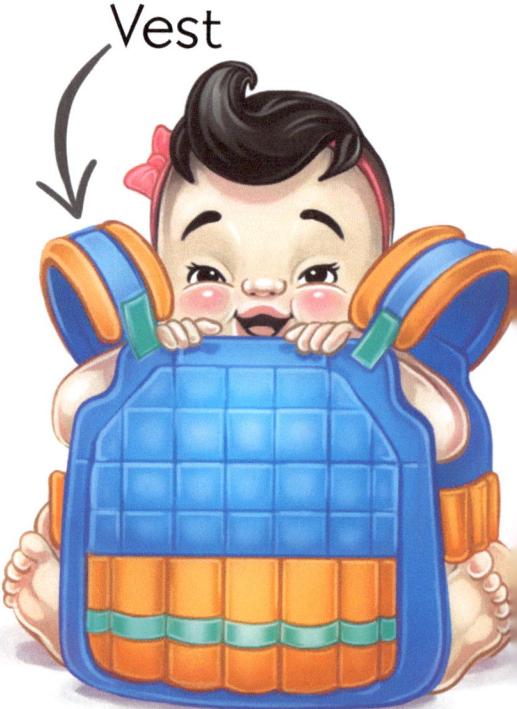

Vest

Ww is for:

Wrist Wraps

Wednesday

Warm-Up
World's Greatest Stretch

WOD
50 Wall Ball Shots
50 Weighted Squats

Skill: Handstand Walks

White Board

Wall Ball

Weights

Water

Xx is for:

E**x**treme

E**x**tra Awesome

E**x**ercise

x Factor

Yy is for:

Yes you can!

Y.B.F.
You'll Be Fine

Prone Y's

Zz is for:

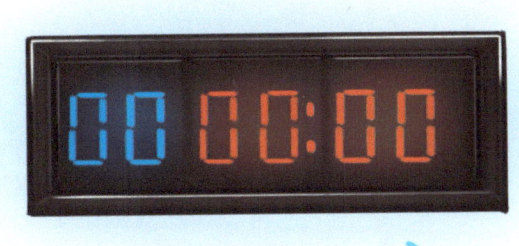

Zero time left!

Now I know my **ABC's** next time won't you ...

WOD
with me?

CPSIA information can be obtained
at www.ICGtesting.com
Printed in the USA
BVHW012315030123
655465BV00002B/50